365 pep talks
from Buddha

365 pep talks
from Buddha

robert allen

6th avenue books™

Introduction

The title of this book caused us no little trouble. The idea was to put into one volume an anthology of thoughts from various sources that would be useful and informative for Buddhists and non-Buddhists alike. "Sermons" certainly didn't seem like the word we wanted (although you do see it used in Western Buddhist literature). What we needed was something that suggested help and encouragement to spiritual seekers rather than orders given to a bunch of raw recruits. We hope that Pep Talks strikes the right note. Although this is a book about Buddhism it has drawn from a variety of religious traditions: Hindu, Taoist, Christian,

Jewish, and Muslim. Buddhism is a very broad church and, in an important sense, there is really no such thing as a Buddhist. If I meet someone on my path and one of us helps the other, then we are both Buddhists, even if one of us happens to be wearing a yamulke or a cross around his neck. Buddhism is no more and no less than a search for liberation. How you get there and whom you travel with are side issues. In an era when religious toleration is having an even tougher time of it than usual perhaps it's useful to remember that we all travel the same road and never know whose help we'll need further along the path.

1

seeking the way

Buddhism isn't an instruction manual, it's a map.

2

a little knowledge

Knowing while thinking you do not know is best. If you think you know but do not, that leads to problems.

LAO-TZU

3

a bit of a stew

A Japanese lord was out hunting when he got separated from his followers and became lost. Eventually, tired and hungry, he reached the hut of an old peasant woman who sat out front cooking a pot of stew.

"I'll give you anything you ask if you let me rest in your hut and eat some of that stew," said the lord.

"You've got nothing I want," replied the old woman.

"I have money," said the lord.

"What use is that to me. Do you see any shops around here?"

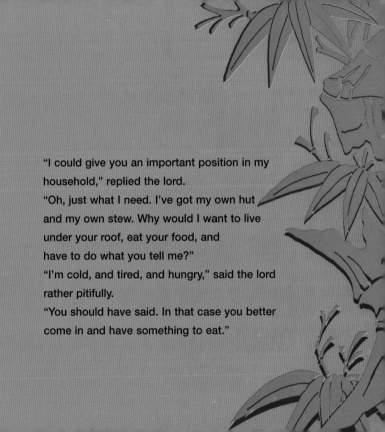

"I could give you an important position in my household," replied the lord.

"Oh, just what I need. I've got my own hut and my own stew. Why would I want to live under your roof, eat your food, and have to do what you tell me?"

"I'm cold, and tired, and hungry," said the lord rather pitifully.

"You should have said. In that case you better come in and have something to eat."

4

baby buddhist

I was a Buddhist long before I knew what a
Buddhist was. There were two things that I was
aware of from my earliest years. One was a sense
of unreality. I have always felt the world is not what
it seems. It's a bit like when you watch a movie
but know that what you're seeing is a clever trick.
The other thing is more important but harder to
describe. I always felt there was an "It" that was
almost visible but just out of reach. "It" wasn't God,
but when I heard about the Way, I knew that was
what I had been searching for.

5

start looking

Buddhism is not passive. It's not like learning
physics or mathematics. Once you start to seek
for it, Buddhism will start to seek for you.

6

experience

Experience is not what happens to you,
it's what you do with what happens to you.

ALDOUS HUXLEY

7

advice

Whoever gives advice to the ignorant
is himself in need of advice.

8

the self

This above all. To thine own self be true,
And it must follow, as night follows day, Thou
canst not then be false to any man.

SHAKESPEARE

life storms

People say, "Into every life some rain must fall." We all know it's true. Sometimes it's not just a light shower but a real downpour. One test of your religion is how it helps you to cope with these events. If you just get your Buddhism from a book you'll find that it helps no more than any other set of platitudes. It all sounds worthy enough but, come the crunch, it won't help much. Meditation is at the heart of Buddhism. This is the treasure house that will enrich your understanding of what Buddhism is all about. If you open this treasure house you will find you have enough resources to overcome any crisis.

10

unhelpful buddha

If you think of a Buddha, that
Buddha will obstruct you!

HUANG PO

11
home arrest

If you regard your home as your most precious possession, then it is no longer a home but a prison. Your home is just another place you are passing through. It serves its turn and then it is gone. Your journey continues without it.

why say sorry?

If you come from a Judaeo-Christian background you'll have the idea of forgiveness firmly planted in your mind. Throw it out! Buddha is not God. He has no power to forgive sins. According to the law of karma, all acts have consequences for their perpetrators. There is no way a bad act can be "forgiven" and a good act carries its own reward. If someone sins against you your forgiveness is irrelevant, though it is important for you that you do not compound this person's error by attaching anger to it and dragging yourself into a train of bad karma.

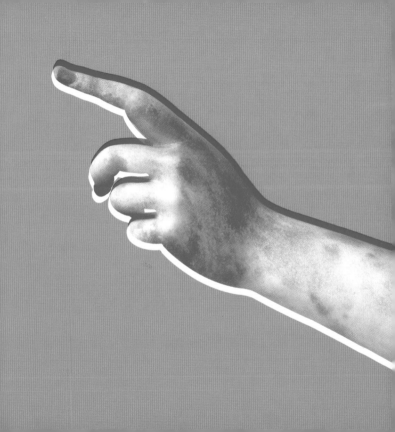

13

route planner

When you choose the beginning of a road
you also choose the destination.

14

make mistakes

Buddhism is a journey into uncharted territory.
You inevitably make mistakes. This is a good thing.
Eventually you will find your way. If you don't risk
taking the odd wrong turn you will go nowhere.

15

great perseverance

There are many accounts of instant enlightenment. What you may not realize is that to reach that stage took many years of effort. You need to be prepared to try, and try, and try even though all your trying is useless. In fact there is nothing you can do to get enlightenment. But if you don't try you'll never get anywhere. Once you have worn out all the options, only then will you be ready for lightning to strike.

16

point of view

As the hand held before the eye conceals the greatest mountain, so the little earthly life hides from the glance the enormous lights and mysteries of which the world is full, and he who can draw it away from before his eyes, as one draws away a hand, beholds the great shining of the inner worlds.

RABBI NACHMAN

dhamapada

The teaching of the Dhamapada (one of the scriptures) are
some of the oldest in Buddhism and are often believed to
be the words of Buddha himself. They read like the moral
equivalent of a cold shower, and that is their value.
Buddhism can get complicated and you may get so
involved in it that you lose sight of the simple things.
Always have a copy of the Dhamapada nearby. It's
uncomfortable reading and will remind you of all the
things you get wrong—but someone has to do it.

18
knee-jerk reaction

An old monk had an arthritic knee but was unable to get treatment. Someone asked him how he put up with the constant pain.

"Oh, it's quite useful really. It's surprising how it puts all your other problems into perspective."

19

the value of happiness

Just because happiness is free
don't think it is worthless.

the cradle of zen

A certain carpenter was said to be a Zen adept. One day a local man asked him to make a cradle for his new baby and the carpenter agreed. A week later the man went to see how the work was coming on, but the carpenter said he was not yet happy with the result. Another week went but, and another, and many more. Still the work was not finished. Eventually the baby grew up to be a man and his wife was about to give birth. He remembered the story of the cradle and went to see if he could get it from the carpenter. "Get lost!" cried the carpenter. "Am I to rush this job just to satisfy the desires of your family?"

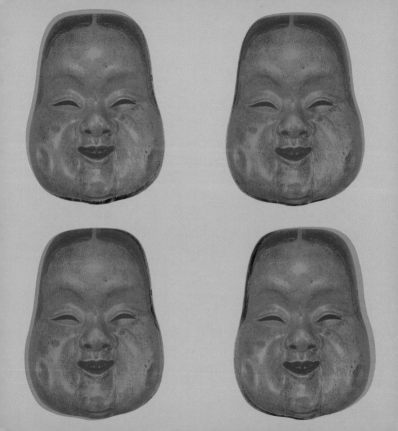

ways to meditate

There are many ways to meditate. The koan, a question unanswerable by logical deduction, has become well known but, for those without a teacher, it is hard to use. Since there is no "right" answer, how will you know when you've solved your koan? Mantras are also popular, though a lot of nonsense is talked about their secret powers. The best form of meditation for the self-taught is simple shikan taza, or following the breath. It may seem rather plain and unexciting but it is all the more powerful for that. Just sit and follow your breathing. Keep focussing your mind on it. At first you may find it boring and pointless but, eventually, you will realize that your breath is about a lot more than just oxygenating your blood.

22

the light

A lamp is invisible in the light of the sun.

All our knowledge cannot compete with enlightenment.

know yourself

To know yourself is the hardest thing,
but also the most important. How do you
know that the self you know is the real self?
The Zen koan asks, "What was your original
face before your parents were born?"

wooden wisdom

A monk was on his way to visit a famous Buddhist teacher. When he got near the master's house he spotted a sign saying "Eating the trees is forbidden." He was puzzled but as he arrived at the front door the master came out to meet him.

"The answer to what puzzles you is that when you feel the same way about greed, lust, anger, and delusion as you do about eating the trees, you'll have gained some wisdom."

25

teachers

If you choose a teacher, choose with care. Is the teacher there to help you, or are you there to help the teacher? People who want to lead a group of disciples are not good teachers. A good teacher tries to push you on so that you can eventually fend for yourself.

26

the pointing finger

Even the greatest teachers do
not preach the truth but only
point the way.

27

no blinding flash

Enlightenment is often spoken of as though it
arrives in a blinding flash like lightning. This is not
always so. The Zen teacher Dogen warned that you
should not necessarily expect to be aware of your
own enlightenment.

28

patience

If you attempt to be a Buddha overnight you'll just
be a very competent hypocrite. Character is built
little by little, day by day.

the others

If you are a Buddhist you embrace the followers of other religions without question. Buddhist teaching is called "dharma," which means law and, like the law of gravity, it is not really open to discussion. That does not mean that you should have an arrogant, "we're right and you're wrong" attitude. It means that you should ignore arguments over dogma and seek to respond to others as fellow beings on a quest for salvation. There are many paths, and they all have the same destination.

me, myself, and I

Think about yourself. How many times have you changed your appearance, your opinions, your job, your partner, or dozens of other things about yourself? Yet you are always sure that you are "you." This flickering, fickle, ever-changing mythical creature is, you believe, as solid and dependable as a rock. Or maybe not?.

31

step by step

Review your life regularly and decide how you could change it for the better. Grand resolutions to reform rarely work, but careful improvement step by step does.

dogged perseverance

There is a story of a dog that, desperately thirsty, went to a pond to drink. Just as it was about to slake its thirst it was frightened by the appearance of another dog in the water and ran away. Its thirst was so great, however, that it kept coming back to see if the "other" dog had gone. Eventually its plight was so desperate that it rushed to the pond and threw itself at its enemy. Then, at last, the dog was saved.

33

want a drink?

Zen is sometimes said to be like selling water by a river. People like to think there is something mysterious and "mystical" about Zen, but there really isn't. Give the arm of your chair a whack with your hand. That's Zen—just exactly what is in front of you right now.

34

soup saying

Even if a fool lives his whole life among the wise he will perceive the truth as little as a spoon perceives the taste of soup.

CHINESE PROVERB

35

the green-eyed god

There are all sorts of jealousy but by far
the oddest is the "They're more spiritually
advanced than me, damn it!" syndrome.
Buddhists are generally very nice people
but the ones who work hard and take their
meditation seriously can get competitive.
If they're not careful they start to compare
notes, each hoping to discover a glimmer

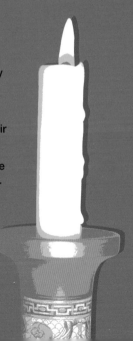

of insight that the others don't yet possess. It's also tempting to want to be the teacher's best pupil and, if you're not, to envy the one who is. Everyone knows they shouldn't feel like this, but just because you know it's wrong doesn't mean it won't happen. It's best to keep at the back of your mind the thought that anyone who feels spiritually advanced isn't.

36
traveling

Don't be impatient. The journey is long, but you have already arrived. Every step of the way brings you closer to where you are right now. When you arrive you will know the place as it really is.

a night on the bare zen mountain

Some think that if they go and live on a mountain like some hermit in a Zen tale they will become enlightened. No way. Stay home, look after your family, walk the dog, wash the dishes, mow the lawn. This is where you'll find enlightenment.

38

buddha miles

"Merit" is an idea that you find in many areas of Buddhism. It involves performing certain acts so that you accumulate points; a bit like Air Miles but more spiritual. Eventually you get to cash in your merit for a better reincarnation. Isn't that stupid? Do good or don't do it, but whatever you do don't count it.

churchgoing

Hatless, I take off
My cycle clips in awkward reverence.

PHILIP LARKIN

the best

Better than sovereignty over the earth, better than the heaven state, better than dominion over all the worlds is the first step on the path to holiness.

DHAMAPADA

41

never mind

It's ten years since I went out of my mind. I'd
never go back.

KEN DODD (BRITISH COMEDIAN)

42

madness

Madness need not be all breakdown.
It may also be breakthrough.

R.D. LAING

43

hara

To meditate properly you need to find your hara. This is a spot below the navel. It has no Western name because science does not acknowledge such an entity. Even so you will be able to feel it. Try to breath from this point and you will soon start to feel it generating a type of energy. This is chi, another thing that "doesn't exist." Once you set this process going your meditation will improve rapidly.

檀香

44

the path

Buddhas do but point the way.
You must tread the path for yourself.

time to get going

Awakening begins when a man
realizes that he is going nowhere and
does not know where to go.

GURDJIEFF

sound and fury

Two monks were disputing an obscure point of the dharma. One began to get angry and, as he made his points, his voice got louder and louder. At last the other said, "I admit that your arguments are sound." Satisfied, the belligerent monk walked off. "Nothing but sound," muttered the other monk to himself.

new bodies for old

Most Buddhists believe that as long as you have desires you will need a body. The body is the home of desire. As long as you need a body you will need to be reborn. Bodies don't last forever and, when one wears out, if you have not yet extinguished desire, you'll need another.

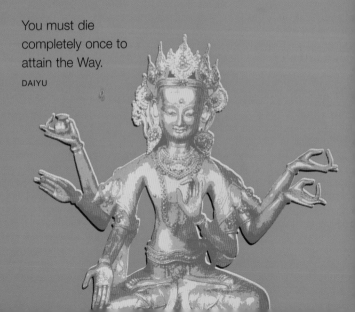

48

seeking death

You must die
completely once to
attain the Way.

DAIYU

bad words

One of the duties of a Buddhist is Right Speech. I used to know a rather prissy young man called Nathan who, every time someone let off some steam, would say reproachfully, "Bad words hurt my ears." Although Nathan was self-righteous and annoying he did have a point. When I was young, nice, educated adults didn't swear except under extreme provocation and never in mixed company. Now almost everyone swears horribly all the time and not for any good reason but just as sort of verbal decoration. The swearing isn't harmless.

The increasing violence of language leads to people thinking and acting more aggressively. Sometimes I've managed to cut out swearing altogether and, amazingly, my thinking has become gentler and kinder straight away. It's easy to slide back into bad habits but the result of speaking calmly and civilly is well worth the effort.

50
books

In the West we have no Buddhist tradition so, if you want to find out about it, you need books. But they can only tell you about Buddhism, they can never give you one atom of the actual experience. The knack is to know at what point to chuck all the books away and simply live Buddhism.

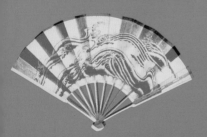

51

mind weeds

Have you ever noticed that it takes hard work to cultivate flowers but weeds come without any effort on your part? It's the same with character. Building a good character takes time and constant effort, a bad character comes easily.

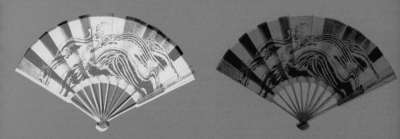

scared to change

Although people think they want enlightenment, they are also scared of it. There is a famous story of a student who described himself as like a dog sitting by a pot of stew. The stew was too hot to eat, but the smell was too tempting to leave! People feel that though their ordinary life brings them pain, at least it is familiar and, in a strange way, safe. What will enlightenment bring? This is an odd way of thinking. As you progress along the road you still remain you. You are not about to turn into someone else. You already are the Buddha you will become.

The mightiest tree will break before a strong enough wind. No wind will ever break the supple bamboo.

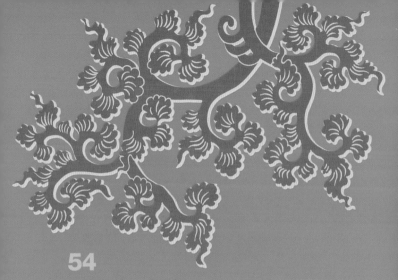

54

friends and foes

Instead of plotting to defeat your enemies, try to find ways to persuade them from their enmity.

no hiding place

Buddhist take refuge in the Buddha.
But he can't help them. They take
refuge in the teaching. But that can't
help them. They take refuge in the
community of monks and nuns. But
they can't help them either. Throw
out all the rubbish, wash off all the
dirt, then sit and watch. When you
reach a place that has no name,
when religion is just a mouthful of
air, you will understand.

56

drowning

Drowning people famously clutch at
straws. But they also clutch at possible
rescuers, which is why lifesavers are
taught to avoid that potentially fatal grip.
Buddhism is just the same—you can't
save people if you let them drag you
down with them.

objections to the objective

People use "subjective" to mean that which is personal, idiosyncratic, or just plain wrong. "Objective" is supposed to mean that which is scientific, provable, confirmed by the observations of others. Yet everything exists for you only in your own mind. That which is not in your mind cannot exist. You cannot even imagine anything that is not in your mind. So where does "objectivity" come into it?

58

travel tip

A rocky road makes hardy travelers.

59

harmony

"How does a man set himself in harmony with
the Tao?" "I am already out of harmony."

SHIH-T'OU

the unlucky ten thousand

When the Great Wall of China was built the emperor was advised by his ministers to sacrifice 10,000 men and bury them under the foundations so that their souls might protect the wall. Even the emperor baulked at the idea of such a massacre, so he found one unfortunate man called Mr. Ten Thousand and had him sacrificed. The emperor felt well satisfied with his own great wisdom and humanity.

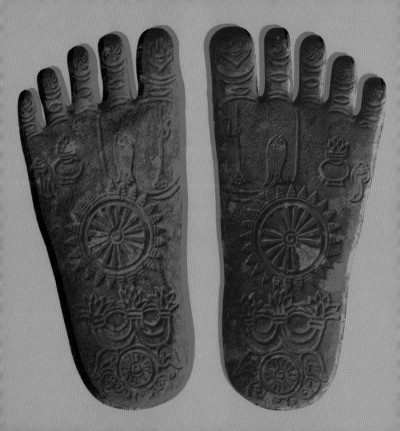

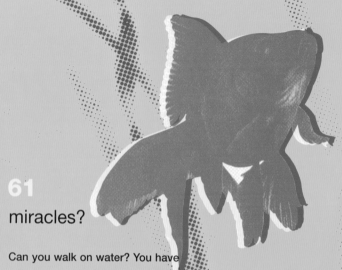

61

miracles?

Can you walk on water? You have
done no better than a straw. Can you
fly in the air? You have done no better
than a bluebottle. Conquer your heart;
then you may become somebody.

ANSARI OF HERAT

mustard seed

When Buddha was asked to perform a
miracle and restore the life of a dead child
he replied by asking the mother to fetch a
mustard seed from a house where no one
had ever died. This was, of course,
impossible. Buddhism has never been
keen on miracles. This world, when truly
appreciated, is the only miracle we need.

Buddhism 24/7

To be of any use to you your Buddhism needs to be 24/7. That doesn't mean that you should spend all your time thinking about "religion." Buddhism has very little to do with what most people think of as religion. But you need to consider your life carefully. Nothing is unimportant, nothing is "just ordinary." Miracles and wonders surround you on all sides. Enlightenment is crowding around trying to attract your attention. Look!

good carpentry

People are like wood, much better to work
with the grain.

no satisfaction

You will make progress in Buddhism but should never
feel satisfied. Just as great musicians and artists
always struggle to improve their skill, Buddhists must
always work to realize the truth.

66
foreign religions

Some people feel that you shouldn't mess with "foreign religions" and should "stick with your own tradition." Although some are attracted to Buddhism because they like the fancy-dress aspects, many find that, far from feeling as though they have discovered something exotic, they feel that they have come home. There is nothing "foreign" about Buddhism; it is just as applicable in modern London or New York as it was in ancient India, China, or Japan. It is about your situation now and, when Buddhist masters taught, they were speaking directly to you.

67

practice

Buddhists call meditation "practice" and it's one of the most important tools for building understanding. It's worth more than all the books, discussions, and sermons in the world. Just sit and do it without expecting anything.

68

the end of opinions

Don't seek reality, just put an end
to opinions.

SHENG-TS'AN

the devil

If you have not seen the devil, look at yourself.

JALAL-UDDIN RUMI

partially sighted

If we do not always see our own mistakes and omissions we can always see those of our neighbors.

71

everyone's a buddha

It is easy to accept the theory that everyone is a Buddha in the making. In practice it is hard. People, including ourselves, behave in all sorts of stupid, selfish, and violent ways so that it's difficult to think of them as Buddhas. Yet we have to make that effort. We have to look for that spark in everyone that makes him or her potentially enlightened. It's surprising that, once you force yourself to look, you start to find it more and more.

reaping what you sow

It's not only individuals who have karma.
It applies to entire nations as well. Where nations
become locked in mutual hatred they breed bad
karma like dung breeds flies. Even the whole of
humanity has its own karma, and the destruction of
the environment suggests that it is in bad shape.

head first

A rotting fish stinks from the head.

POLISH PROVERB

attachment

If we cling to things like money, possession, and fame, these will cause us pain in due course. Sensible people see this easily. But what about "good" attachments? We love our partner, our children, our home. Yet, eventually, we must lose all these. Life is nothing but change. This is one of the hardest things for us to accept. This is why the earliest Buddhists became monks and rid themselves of all attachments. It is a burden that nearly all modern Buddhists must learn to carry.

75

don't be a stranger

Weeds choke up an unused path. Go often to the important places in your life.

76

stream of consciousness

You cannot step into the same river twice.
And it isn't just the river that's changed.

77

location of happiness

The city of happiness is in the state of mind.

78

just smile

Smile! No one is so foreign, so young, or so old that they will not understand you.

illusion

When you start to meditate
strange things may happen. These
can be pleasant or unpleasant. Gods,
demons, and strange creatures may smile or leer at
you from anywhere. You may experience a variety of
odd sensations. All these are nothing but illusion.
Ignore them, they mean nothing and, eventually,
they will cease completely.

save yourself

There's no point trying to rush around "saving" people. Save them from whom? Save them for what? Who are you to save anyone anyway? The only person you can work on is yourself, and by doing that you save everyone. Only this way will you know what that really means.

happiness

If your religion does not make you happier, more peaceful, more contented, then you're doing it wrong.

82

the gift of the giver

Lieh-tzu's fame as a man of Tao reached
the ears of a government minister who,
hearing that he lived a life of poverty, sent
a gift of food. Lieh-tzu bowed deeply but
declined the gift.
"Why did you do that?" complained his
wife, "We needed that food."
"He only sent it because one of his staff
aroused his sense of duty, not because
he has any love for the Way. You can't
go accepting gifts from people like that."

LIEH-TZU

83

learning

To learn it is necessary to discover the depths of our own ignorance.

limits of knowledge

You realize how little you know when a child
begins to ask questions.

so much compassion

People often lament the fact that there is so little compassion in the world and that humans are so capable of cruelty. The really remarkable fact is that there is so much compassion. People will make sacrifices to help those who are homeless and starving in places they have barely heard of. They will willingly give food to creatures of another species, even when they don't intend to eat them later! Compassion and kindliness are not like rare exotic flowers, they are the daisies of the human mind.

bittersweet

If you are bitter at heart, sugar in the mouth
won't help you.

JEWISH PROVERB

learning in old age

Anyone who is too old to learn was probably
always too old to learn.

bringing home the bacon

One Buddhist duty is Right Livelihood. I think it means more than just not becoming a bank robber or a slaughterhouse worker. I think it means that you have to think about what you are doing with your time. Many workers may lead entirely blameless lives at work but be so busy with everyday matters that their attention is diverted from their spiritual development. You can't leave out a whole chunk of your day and keep it separate. If you're a Buddhist, then everything you do is part of your practice.

89

twice as wrong

A man who makes a mistake but does
not correct it is making another mistake.

CONFUCIUS

90
keeping focused

If you keep your heart transparent
you will never be bound.
But one disturbing thought creates
ten thousand distractions.
If you let many things capture your
attention you'll go astray.
How painful it is to see people so
wrapped up in themselves!

RYOKAYAYANA

91

great faith

Buddhist faith is not like that of other religions. You are not required to believe anything without first proving it to your own satisfaction. But you do need to be confident that our way does eventually lead to enlightenment. That confidence is frequently tested, especially before understanding starts to grow. Without it you will never last long enough to see the results of your labor.

zen diet

A young man went to a Zen master to ask to
become his pupil.
"Go home," said the master, "and eat only a
little plain rice each day. After a week have a
sumptuous meal prepared for you and your
family. If you can then leave and come back
here without eating that meal I'll teach you."

making repairs

You repair your house, you have your car serviced, you refrigerate your food, and you look after your body, getting exercise when you're well and going to the doctor when you're sick. But what about the mind? It often gets overlooked. Because we are "in" it all the time, we take it for granted. Yet nothing is more important. Buddhism provides servicing and repair for the mind, and you can get upgrades as well!

94

too much

Tie two birds together and
they will be unable to fly
even though they have twice
the number of wings.

SUFI SAYING

95
double act

Buddhism and Taoism are not at all the same thing. Even so they are kissing cousins and, had that not been so, Zen would never have been born. Without Taoism, Buddhism is like popcorn without the toffee.

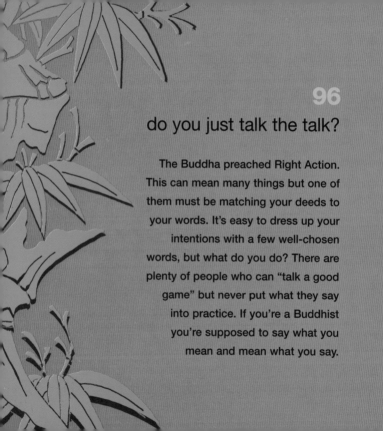

do you just talk the talk?

The Buddha preached Right Action. This can mean many things but one of them must be matching your deeds to your words. It's easy to dress up your intentions with a few well-chosen words, but what do you do? There are plenty of people who can "talk a good game" but never put what they say into practice. If you're a Buddhist you're supposed to say what you mean and mean what you say.

water

Buddhists and Taoists often talk about water as an example of how to behave. Water does good, but claims no credit, it takes only the lowest position for itself and, though it appears to be soft, it can wear away rock.

the law of averages

Karma is not about averages. A good act has good consequences; a bad act has bad consequences. Neither can be avoided. And be careful, karma can be tricky and unpredictable. Don't miss an opportunity to do good, but think before you act.

99

just mad about monks

If you read much Buddhist literature you'd be forgiven for thinking that your only course, if you want to be a real Buddhist, is to enter a monastery. Theravadin Buddhism (the oldest variety) in particular seems to suggest that the only life worth living is that of a monk or nun. So, are you going to join up? Almost certainly not. Does this make you a second-rate Buddhist? No, it doesn't. Buddhism is not fixed in one period of time; it grows and develops. What was acceptable in ancient China or Japan is not acceptable now. What's more, the change is for the better. Leading a holy life in the seclusion of a monastery seems a pretty poor option. Buddhism is about all life. Surely it's best to get out there and be a Buddhist in the real world, coming to terms with its distractions and temptations.

go with the flow

As long as you think you understand, you don't. As long as you think you can put a single foot safely on the ground, you can't. The point of Buddhism is to let go of all the things you mistakenly think are supporting you. Just like someone learning to swim finds that water, almost unbelievably, supports a human body, so life supports a free mind.

101
beauty and truth

True speech is not beautiful
Beautiful speech is not true.

TAO TE CHING

taking the precepts

In Thailand, where I had my early experience of Buddhism, it is the custom to "take the precepts" by promising to keep them strictly for a certain length of time (a week is common). If you come from a Christian background this may sound odd. Surely you should keep the Commandments all the time. But do you? Probably not; taking the precepts is much tougher than it sounds. Try it.

103

soul stirring

The soul is no more in the body
than the body is in the soul.

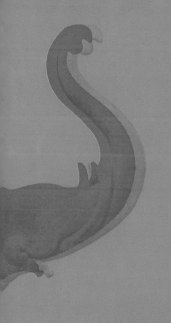

104

don't let your meditation become a habit

Some say that meditation should be
a habit like cleaning your teeth.
Nothing could be more useless. Each
meditation is special and unique.
Never let it become a habit.

a sense of unreality

Because we have always known the world as it is, we assume that it is ordinary, normal, okay. But have you really looked at it recently? Think, for example, about time. What is it? Where does it come from? Where does it go? You can study physics until you're blue in the face but you won't discover anything that dispels the notion that the world is, in fact, very odd indeed. Once you are no longer fooled into thinking everything is "normal," you are ready to look life full in the face.

106

within and without

There is no place that is
outside of God.

ANONYMOUS

where do you think you're going?

Whereas originally Buddhism aimed to end human suffering, I think that for many of us the aim has changed. People who see the oddness of our existence and are fascinated by it are keen to find out what is going on. Buddhism offers an excellent method of doing this. It presents people with an unparalleled opportunity for exploration and discovery. It also helps you to sort out your life but, for many, the sheer joy of discovery outweighs personal advantage.

covert no one

Don't waste time trying to convert your friends to Buddhism. Religious enthusiasts can be considered bores and cranks. If you show them by your example that this is a good way to lead your life, that's good. Maybe they'll want to copy you. Otherwise keep your mouth shut.

109

the self

Learn to look with an equal eye upon
all beings, seeing the one Self in all.

SRIMAD BHAGAVATAM

110

no gradual way

Enlightenment is sudden and complete.
It does not come to us bit by bit. Though
understanding increases over time, that
is not the same thing as enlightenment.
Fruit grows riper on the tree but there is
only one moment at which it falls.

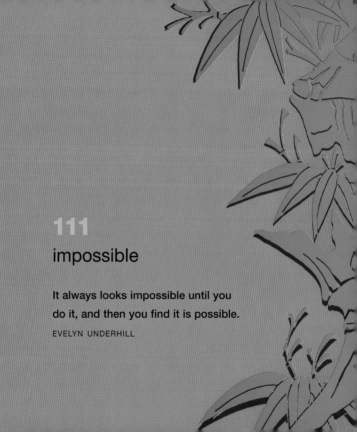

111

impossible

It always looks impossible until you
do it, and then you find it is possible.

EVELYN UNDERHILL

monkey zen

I'd been reading a Japanese swordsman's thoughts on "not stopping the mind." This is a key Zen concept that I'd never really understood. Then I happened to visit a zoo and had the matter explained to me beautifully by a monkey that dropped from a high branch down a series of lower branches to the floor. A human would have seen this as a series of awkward maneuvers to be undertaken with great care and one at a time. The monkey saw the whole thing as being all of a piece. It was perfectly clear that in the monkey's mind it had landed even before it took off. Even a monkey can be an excellent Zen teacher.

113
learning to ride

Buddhism isn't an arm-round-the-shoulder-sympathy sort of religion. It's more like learning to ride a bike. Push off, pedal like hell, and every time you fall off get back on and try again.

folk wisdom

Most folks are as happy as they
make up their mind to be.

ABRAHAM LINCOLN

the best quality

Some friends got hold of one of those Internet questionnaires that do the rounds and we all filled it in. One of the instructions was: "Say something nice about the person who sent you this." Discussing it afterward I asked one of my friends what the nicest thing was that anyone had said about her. At first she wouldn't tell but, after much persuasion, she admitted the remark that had meant most to her had been: "She has integrity."

fresh looking

It is hard to look at things with fresh eyes. As we get older we tend to rely on experience but that often means we don't really see what's in front of us, just what we think we saw last time. But to be a Buddhist you must learn to look afresh. Our familiar world is much more than it seems and, unless you look closely, you'll miss it.

117

the beauty of mystery

The most beautiful thing we can
experience is the mysterious. It is
the source of all true art and all
science. He to whom this emotion
is a stranger, who can no longer
pause to wonder and stand rapt
in awe, is as good as dead:
his eyes are closed.

ALBERT EINSTEIN

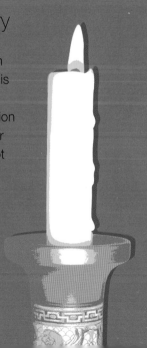

IQ

For some reason Zen has got the image of being difficult and, because of this, a lot of highly educated and intelligent people think it is just the sort of Buddhism for them. This is odd because it's not possible to intellectualize your way through Zen. It's like having a thorough knowledge of the history, development and theory of windsurfing without ever having actually stood on a surfboard.

119

attitude problem

People will pick up on your mental attitude even when you
say nothing. Just by being calm, peaceable, and kindly you
will be helping others, whether you are aware of it or not.
By the same token, if you are angry and filled with hatred
you will give rise to great harm even if you never
say or do anything.

daring

There are those who are so scrupulously
afraid of doing wrong that they seldom
venture to do anything.

VAUVENARGUES

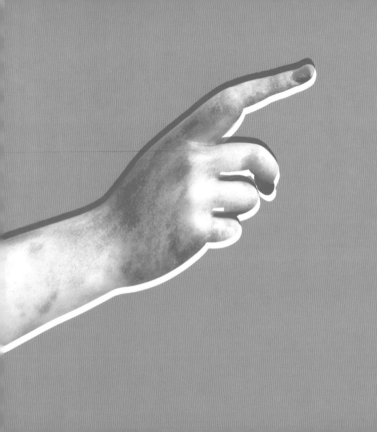

open up

When you meditate don't make the mistake of trying to shut the world out. All the distracting sounds coming from outside are actually part of your meditation. Expand your mind, include everything, birds singing, children playing, even cars that pass in the street. There is nothing that is not Buddha and there is nothing that should not be part of meditation.

122

hidden thoughts

Do not think that there is a part of your mind that is secret, personal, and belongs to just you. The world is your thoughts, all of them. When you harbor hatred and desire these things are as much a part of the world as a tree or a large rock. That is why it is necessary to watch what you think.

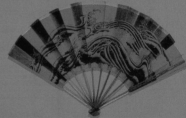

123

going off slowly

An evil deed, like freshly drawn milk,
does not turn sour at once.

DHAMAPADA

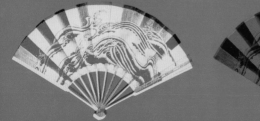

award for industry

When the Zen master Hakuin was a junior monk he went on a journey with some of his superiors. As he was young and vigorous the elder monks got him to carry their luggage. He did so willingly and made the carrying of the luggage a useful opportunity to meditate. By the time they arrived at their destination he was exhausted. The next part of the journey was by boat and, once they were on board, Hakuin curled up in a corner and fell fast asleep. During the voyage a storm sprung up and everyone on board got seasick, except Hakuin who remained fast asleep until after the storm was over.

great doubt

Doubting is one of the great things about Buddhism. Doubt everything! Always! Never be satisfied with how things look on the surface. Dig deep and you will see that life is not at all as you imagined. This should be a constant habit.

126

appearances

Things are not as they seem—
and nor are they otherwise.

LANKAVATARA SUTRA

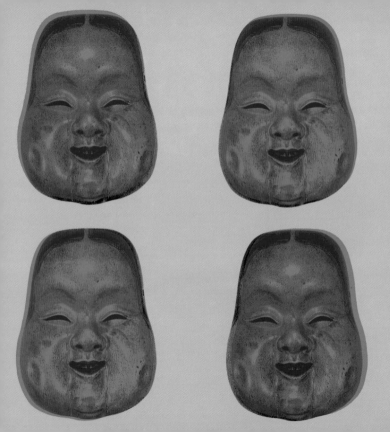

nowhere to tread

People seek the truth the way they would pick a path
through a swamp. They tread gingerly, testing to see
where it is safe to set foot. But there is no safe path.
There is nowhere to set foot. As long as you seek the
path you cannot find it. Abandoning the path while you
are in a swamp takes courage. It is not to be attempted
straight away. Slowly you will realize that the things you
tried to rest upon will not support you for long.
Eventually you will come to see that you were never
in danger of sinking at all.

128

good and bad

The good, I treat as good. Those who are not good I also treat as good. That way I gain in goodness. Those who are of good faith, I have faith in. Those who are not of good faith I also have faith in. That way I gain in good faith.

TAO TE CHING

129

existence

There's never been a single thing,
So where's defiling dust to cling?

HUI NENG

130
no smoking!

A Zen monk was on his travels visiting various temples to increase his understanding. On his way someone gave him a pipe and tobacco. He found that smoking, especially after a hard day's walking, was very pleasant. But then he realized that it was distracting him from his efforts to attain enlightenment and he threw the smoking kit away.

131

the way of the world

Life and death are great mysteries.
The more we discover the more we
find out that we don't know. Nothing
is ever certain. Should we despair?
No, it all seems to work very well
indeed without our help.

132

chew

Chew every mouthful thirty times
When I was a child we were told to chew every
mouthful of food thirty times. Needless to say,
no one did. Nonetheless chewing your life
thoroughly is a good idea. Just as the object of a
good meal is to savor it rather than gulp it down
in a hurry, life is a whole lot more fascinating if
you take time to enjoy it bit by bit.

a passion for compassion

As your practice advances your compassion grows deeper. That's great. But nothing in Buddhism is straightforward. Even compassion can become an attachment. Suppose you spend so much time rushing about saving the world that you no longer practice. What then? Buddhism is not about politics or social reform. It's about enlightenment.

134
just do it!

Buddhism is something to believe,
it's something to do.

135

no more rules

Boy Scouts have a set of rules to govern their behavior. Traditionally the last one is, "Forget all the others." They have a point. Although Buddhism has all sorts of precepts and advice to stop you going astray, the only thing that really matters is your pursuit of the truth. If you keep that in mind all the time, all the rules will keep themselves.

unlikely teachers

Everyone and everything can be your teacher. It is said that when the student is ready the teacher will appear, but do not suppose he will be a wise old monk in a saffron robe. When you have the right understanding teachers will appear in even the unlikeliest places.

137

here and now

Once you know that Buddhism is really
what is happening every second of every
minute of every day, then you will begin
to understand.

138

labels

Words such as, "enlightenment," "Buddha," "Zen" are merely used for convenience. It is important not to get stuck with names. Really there are no names. What we call Zen is not really Zen and what we call enlightenment is no such thing. When you meditate let yourself go beyond names to that which has no name.

advice to ananda

"Therefore, O Ananda, be ye islands unto yourselves. Take the Self as your refuge. Take yourself to no external refuge. Hold fast to the Dhamma as an island. Hold fast as a refuge to the truth. Look not for refuge to anyone besides yourselves. …And whosoever, Ananda, shall take the island as a refuge, taking themselves to no external refuge, but holding fast to Truth as their refuge, it is they, Ananda, who shall reach the very topmost height—but they must be anxious to learn."

BUDDHA

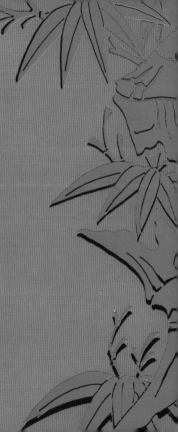

140
lying

To tell lies to others is
foolish; to tell lies to
yourself is a disaster.

141
helping hands

In olden days Buddhism was about masters and pupils. Now a strange thing has happened and, since Buddhism came west, the masters are rare and the students many. Always take time to help others following the way. You will find there is no shortage of people willing to help you.

142
is that a fact?

There are no facts, only interpretations.

NIETZSCHE

reincarnation

Nay, but as when one layeth
His worn out robes away,
And taking new ones, sayeth,
"These will I wear today!"
So putteth by the spirit
Lightly its garb of flesh,
And passeth to inherit
A residence afresh.

THE BHAGAVAD-GITA

144

big questions

What some people think of as the Big Questions
(Why are we here? Where are we going? Is there a
God?), do not concern Buddhists. The only Buddhist
question is "Who am I?" Once you have the answer
to that, you have all that you need.

145

wisdom and strength

To know men is to be wise,
To know yourself is to be illumined.
To conquer men is to have strength,
To conquer yourself is to be even stronger.

TAO TE CHING

enlightenment

A lamp is not used to illuminate itself.

SUFI SAYING

endless desire

Desires are without end. Even when you get
what you want it will fail to satisfy you. Soon
you'll want more, or something different. The
products of desire never satisfy, they just help
to engender more desire. Learn to be content
and you will always have enough.

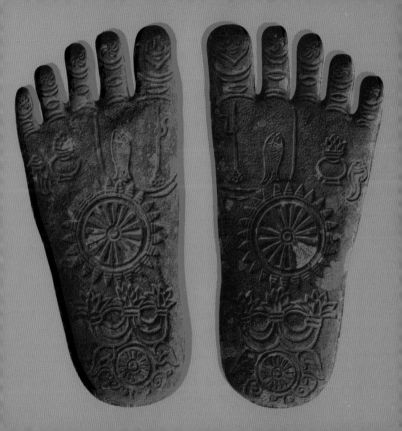

148

buddha sends his converts out into the world

Go ye forth, O Bhikkhus (monks), for the gain of the many, for the welfare of the many, in compassion for the world. Proclaim the Doctrine glorious, preach ye a life of holiness, perfect and pure.

BUDDHA

149
nothing special

Buddhism is not about the foreign, the exotic, the unusual. Buddhism is your ordinary life. Getting up, washing, eating, going to work, these are all Buddhism. Anything else is just a fancy-dress party.

150
each day

This day will not come again. Each day is a priceless gem.

TAKUAN

hard-headed people

There are people who feel that they are just too practical to waste time on Buddhism. They believe that "Eastern mysticism" is vague, foolish, and impractical, whereas money, power, and status are what the world is really all about. Ask yourself, what could possibly be more pointless than these "realities"? The crazy gambling of the stock exchanges, the vagaries of the currency markets, and the power-seeking and lies of the politicians, are these really what life is supposed to be about?

tolerance

Buddhism's greatest gift to the world is
tolerance. This is not always easy to keep up.
Some people are themselves so intolerant that it
is very tempting to pay them back in the same
coin. But remember, for over 2,500 years
Buddhism has managed to avoid intolerance.
Surely you can manage during a lifetime?

153

open-minded

Minds, like parachutes, work only when
they are open.

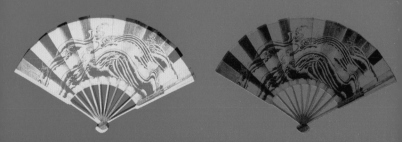

154
no paths

Truth is a pathless land, and you cannot approach it by any path whatsoever, by any religion, by any sect.

KRISHNAMURTI

155

doing good

He who wants to do good
knocks at the door; he who
loves finds the door open.

RABINDRANATH TAGORE

samurai

Like all forms of Buddhism, Zen encourages compassion and the saving of all sentient beings. So why did it attract the samurai? What they liked about it was its spontaneity and wholeheartedness. The samurai weren't people who did anything by halves and they preferred action to theorizing. Zen seeks to outwit the cumbersome, logical one-thing-at-a-time thought processes and discover action that occurs before thinking.

actions speak louder than words

Listen carefully to what people tell you, but look
even more carefully at what they do.

158

just do it!

Disease is not cured by pronouncing the name
of the medicine, but by taking the medicine.
Deliverance is not achieved by repeating the word
"Brahman," but by directly experiencing Brahman.

SHANKARA

fellow travelers

To think of Buddhism as another religion like
Christianity, Judaism, or Islam is to miss the point
entirely. Buddhism is not an exclusive club with a
membership list. It is a group of travelers on the
same journey. Anyone is welcome to join. Anyone
we meet on the road is a companion deserving our
help. There are really no non-Buddhists.

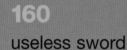

160

useless sword

Just as a sword cannot cut itself, the ego cannot liberate itself. This is why we must use subtle means to achieve liberation.

quality that counts

Long meditation is not a virtue in itself. A short period done well is worth more than many hours done poorly. Make sure you meditate when you feel fresh. If you feel tired, sleep first. Then put everything you've got into it.

162

difficult people

Some people are just plain awkward and difficult to deal with. What do you do? You have to try harder with such people. You won't always win—some people are just not open to persuasion. But, even so, it is important to leave your heart open to them. No one should be excluded; everyone matters in the end.

163

you know what you need

Listen to your own inner voice. You
know what you need. You know the
things you have to do. You know
what you don't need and the
things you shouldn't do.
Learn to trust yourself.

164
drawing conclusions

An American girl sat sketching a huge
Buddha image in the grounds of a Thai
temple. She was concentrating so hard
that she didn't hear an elderly monk
approaching. When she saw him she
became nervous. Maybe sketching was
forbidden. Perhaps she was going to get
told off. But the monk took a look at her
drawing and smiled.

"Seeing his very important," he said. "You
must always look, look, look."

buddha is not a warm puppy

In the West Buddhism tends to attract nice, kindly, liberal-minded folk. That's great because you can never have too many of those people around. The trouble is that they tend to see the Buddha as warm, cuddly, and compassionate. The last is true, but not the first two. Buddhism is really about getting up off your backside and saving yourself.

bite your tongue

Patience is never more important than
when you are on the verge of losing it.

ANONYMOUS

167

foolish fox

A fox that breaks into a hen house might kill a dozen hens but only make off with one. What a fool! Think of the meals he might have enjoyed if he'd been less greedy.

168
end matter

Old age strips bare what we have done with our lives. How much will your achievements count for? What have status and money done for you? It is at death's door that we know who we really are.

169

love hurts

In most religions love is regarded as the highest good. The love we show to others is a pale reflection of the love that God gives to us. Buddhism is different. Love is a form of attachment. Much of what we call love is actually selfish, greedy, and dependent. We hang on to other people desperately because we are afraid of being alone. This does not mean that Buddhists are condemned to a solitary, loveless existence. It means that, like all attachments, it must be recognized for what it is. We can grow into a state where we care for others in a way that is not self-seeking, but it takes thought and a lot of work.

170
advice

Whoever gives advice to the ignorant
is himself in need of advice.

171
learning from karma

Karma punishes the foolish but teaches the wise.

172

the way of the sword

Sometimes students are taught to meditate by visualizing themselves confronted by a swordsman with his weapon drawn. Just a split second of inattention and you lose your head!

giving

Buddhists place great value on giving. This could be just some coins in the charity box, but it is much better to give yourself. You have so many treasures that you could share. Give everything you can.

174

striving for peace

Should you desire great tranquillity,
prepare to sweat white beads.

HAKUIN

habit forming

**A bad habit is first a spider's thread,
then a rope, and finally a chain.**

unlearning

Most religions involve learning. Buddhism is
about unlearning. If you learn a language,
each day you acquire a few words, some
grammar, a better accent. When you learn
Buddhism every day you throw away some
more useless baggage.

177

homeward bound

Buddhism is not about anything strange or exotic. Enlightenment is not about flying off to the stars. Our original nature is already enlightened. Buddhism is about finding our way home.

178

form and substance

There was a young man who took
the Buddhist precepts very seriously. He
never smoked or drank, was scrupulously
honest, gave money and food to the local
temple, and was a good husband and father.
He worked as a public prosecutor and every
day was responsible for poor wretches being
dragged away in chains to a filthy prison.
Going through the motions of Buddhism
without true compassion is as useless as
learning to swim on dry land.

self-satisfaction

Be yourself. If that doesn't
satisfy you, improve yourself.

self love

Remember that your Self is an illusion.
Why fall in love with it?

paper tigers

It is said that Chinese magicians could take a paper cut-out of a tiger and change it into the real thing. The magic tiger was, however, only an illusion. If you faced it with courage it became, like so many of the things we fear, powerless to hurt you. To this day the Chinese refer to a baseless fear as a paper tiger.

182

living in the world

Morality that hides behind monastery walls is a poor thing. The difficult thing is to live in the world and yet not only maintain your values but also strengthen your belief.

183

mind what you think

Your whole life exists only in your mind.
Your body exists in your mind. Your family
exist in your mind. Your home exists in
your mind. Your job exists in your mind. If
these things were not mind objects they
could not exist. Watch your mind!

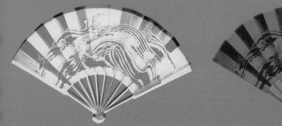

184

a difficult crossing

Few there are among men who
arrive at the other shore; most of them
run up and down this shore.

DHAMAPADA

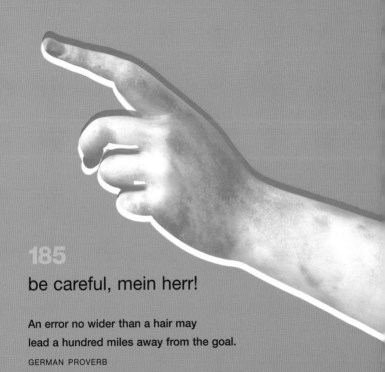

185

be careful, mein herr!

An error no wider than a hair may
lead a hundred miles away from the goal.

GERMAN PROVERB

the lure of lust

The Buddha is supposed to have said, "There is no fire like lust." Religions all seem to have a dim view of sex and Buddhism is no different. It's true that sex can become addictive and lead to all sorts of trouble. But is this a reason why we should all behave like Victorian maiden aunts and throw our arms up in horror at the sight of naked flesh? I think that trying to avoid lust by suppressing it is the road to ruin. Those of us who have been able to express our sexual feelings honestly do eventually arrive at a stage where those feelings transmute into something kinder, gentler, and wiser.

187

living well

The happiest life is lived
for others.

a moment with camus

Every minute of life carries with it miraculous
value, and its face of eternal youth.

ALBERT CAMUS

wrong conduct

Sooner or later, false thinking
brings wrong conduct.

JULIAN HUXLEY

deep virtue

Some virtue is only skin-deep. It's
not just what you do that counts, but
what you would do if you were sure
that you wouldn't be found out.

keep on moving

Meditation goes through many stages. Some of these can be extremely pleasant. You may start to laugh out loud for no reason, or even experience feelings of bliss. It is important not to get enchanted by these feelings so that you try to hang on to them. Let them come and then let them go. If you try to recapture a feeling that you enjoyed you will not be able to make progress. It is a long journey.

192

good teaching

It was the Buddhist patriarch, Dogen, who said that good teaching feels as if something was being forced on us. Often the thing that we need most is hardest to accept. We reject good teaching because it is inconvenient or implies criticism of our present way of life. When such teaching comes, we should make a point of listening carefully.

193

inexplicable

My own suspicion is that the universe is not only queerer than we suppose but queerer than we can suppose.

J.B.S. HALDANE

prize giving

As long as you view enlightenment as a prize
to be won, it will elude you. But if you don't
think of it like that, then why do you want it?
By struggling to grasp it you merely push it
further away. The point is that you are already
enlightened; you only have to realize it.

195

wise fools

Beware—the wise often appear
simple and the simple may try
to appear wise. Only the truly
wise can tell the difference.

196

satori (enlightenment)

It is said that the way to satori is the gateless gate. Yet that no-gate is marked "Push hard."

postcards from heaven

If friends went on vacation and sent you a postcard, how much would you know of the place they'd visited? All religions are like this. They are simply postcards from people who've been there. But if you want to know, you must go yourself.

198

empty sky

The sky is empty; heaven does not speak.

199
enlightenment

Enlightenment is no state. Buddha did
not attain it. Sentient beings do not lack it.
It cannot be reached by body or mind.
All sentient beings have it already.

HUANG PO

200
sex and death

How alike the groans of love to those of the dying.

MALCOLM LOWRY

201
battle of the sexes?

There is no such quality as male and female. In its ultimate nature, every mind is the same.

growth

A tree grows until the moment it is cut down. It is important to be like the tree. Many people stop growing when they marry, when they have children, when they get a good job. Whenever they feel, "Now I've made it and I can have a rest." This is not the way. Like a plant you must try to grow toward the light all the time.

203

the drum

I will beat the drum of the Immortal
in the darkness of the world.

BUDDHA

204

god's day job

It is a mistake to believe that
God is only, or even chiefly,
concerned with religion.

WILLIAM TEMPLE

getting away with it

Many people try to convince themselves that karma doesn't work. They point out that evil people often lead successful lives. But they lead them as evil people! That in itself is a disaster. In truth there is no escape from evil acts though, just as the rain does not always come straight after the thunder, the consequences of evil are not always immediately apparent.

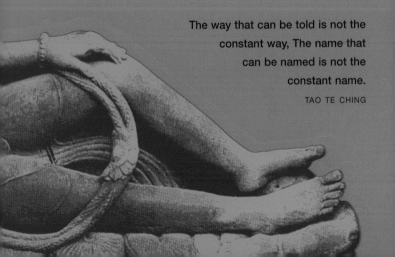

206

strength in weakness

Grass, which is tender and weak, breaks
concrete that is hard and strong.

207

the way

The way that can be told is not the
constant way, The name that
can be named is not the
constant name.

TAO TE CHING

just look

Buddhist monks are sometimes taught just to sit and examine their thoughts. Try it. Don't try to think of anything in particular. Especially don't try to think "good" thoughts. Just look at what you are thinking and take note of it. If you are feeling sad, watch your sadness as though you were a tourist in your own mind. No matter whether you feel angry, or jolly, or envious, or fearful, or loving, or peaceful, just watch how your thoughts arise and how they disappear. You can't hold them! No matter how strongly you feel something it will soon pass away. Even a strong emotion like grief will come and go. Your thoughts are slippery as eels. Just watch how they dart through the waters of the mind.

209

hatred

"He abused me, he beat me, he defeated me, he robbed me"—in those who harbor such thoughts hatred will never cease.

"He abused me, he beat me, he defeated me, he robbed me"—in those who do not harbor such thoughts hatred will cease.

For hatred does not cease by hatred at any time—this is an old rule.

DHAMAPADA

hidden danger

To do what is wrong can seem
so attractive that you forget the
danger. Tigers are beautiful,
but would you pat one?

a matter of image

There are more images of Buddha in the world than of any other person in history. How annoyed he would be! In some places these images are treated with huge respect, kept above head height, touched only with the greatest care, gilded, and given offerings of incense and flowers. Small wonder that the missionaries thought Buddhists were idolaters.

a bump in the night

Our most basic emotion is fear. Think how much time we devote to being afraid. Most of the time is taken up by minor worries like being late for work, or being given a parking ticket. Then we have bigger fears such as injury, illness, bereavement, and death. These big fears usually lurk in the background and only come out to scare us in our dreams. But they are there all the time, waiting for a moment when we are too weak to oppose them. Buddhists believe that this fear is the result of clinging, a refusal to let go and surrender ourselves to our Buddha nature. Like people climbing a mountain, the ones who are most afraid are those most likely to fall. It is no good trying to rationalize such fears away because they are not rational. Regular meditation, however, is the way to help yourself to outgrow them.

one god

Millions believe in the One True God, yet they all have different gods. It isn't God who's confused.

don't bang a gong

Buddhism is not about being Chinese or Japanese or Tibetan. It's not about Buddha images or incense or bells or drums. Buddhism is about you. Now. Wherever you live.

215

between a rock and a hard place

There's a story of a Zen master who never lay down to sleep and, eventually, even died sitting in meditation. The story is usually told in tones of great reverence for this fiercely ascetic monk. But why? I've always felt he needed to get out more.

216

mind and matter

I regard consciousness as
fundamental. I regard matter as
derivatives from
consciousness. We
cannot get behind
consciousness.

MAX PLANK

217

troubled turtle

In China there was a turtle of such immense age that it became famous and was brought to the emperor. The strain of this upheaval was so great that the turtle died. Even so, its shell was ornamented with precious jewels and put on display. A Taoist adept who heard the story commented, "How much happier the turtle would have been if it had been left to wag its tail in the mud."

let poverty be your treasure

Money doesn't talk it swears.

BOB DYLAN

just give

As a full jar overthrown pours out the liquid and keeps back nothing, even so shall your charity be without reserve—as a jar overturned.

BUDDHA

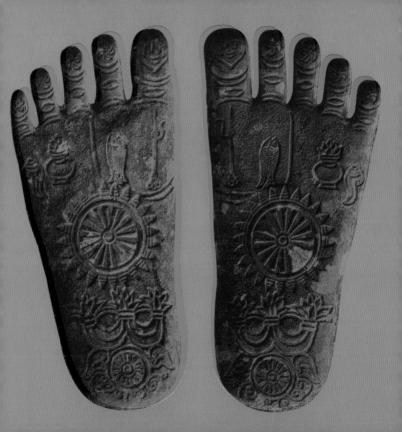

changing the world

Karl Marx memorably said, "Philosophers have interpreted the world in various ways; the point is to change it." Many people have been tempted by the same thought. Wouldn't the world be a great place if only I could reshape it my way? Hitler and Stalin started out thinking that they were making things better. The essence of the world is unchanging and unchangeable. You can tinker with it (and usually make a worse mess) but you can never alter the fundamentals. According with the Way is, eventually, the only way.

give careful thought to this

All that we are is the result of what we have thought: it is founded on our thoughts and is made up of our thoughts.

DHAMAPADA

mind

This mind is no mind of conceptual thought and it is completely detached from form. So Buddhas and sentient beings do not differ at all.

HUANG PO

223

original mind

There is no Buddhist concept equivalent to the Christian idea of original sin. To Buddhists, original mind is pure. We may get deluded, confused, or just plain stupid and, while in such a state, do bad things. But it's just like a child who plays thoughtlessly and gets dirty. The dirt washes off. All it needs is a damn good scrub.

224

be still

You do not need to leave your room. Remain sitting at your table and listen. Do not even listen; simply wait. Do not even wait; be still and solitary. The world will freely offer itself to you to be unmasked; it has no choice. It will roll in ecstasy at your feet.

FRANZ KAFKA

225

sitting

When you sit down to meditate do it as though you will never get up.

going deeper

If we go down into ourselves we find that
we possess exactly what we desire.

SIMONE WEIL

growing to the light

Plants always grow toward the light. They just can't help themselves. People are different, they can choose. Choosing the light isn't easy: it requires constant effort. Most people know what they should do, but doing it takes courage and stamina.

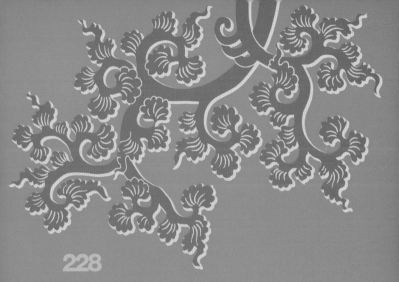

228

lack of understanding

My words are both easy to understand and put into
practice. Even so, there is no one in the whole world
who can understand them or put them into practice.

LAO-TZU

229

awakening doubts

**Great doubt gives rise to great awakening; small
doubt, small awakening; no doubt, no awakening.**
ZEN SAYING

230

difficult teaching

Teaching that feels disagreeable can be
the best teaching. No one likes to learn
what is difficult or painful, but these are
often the lessons that help us most.

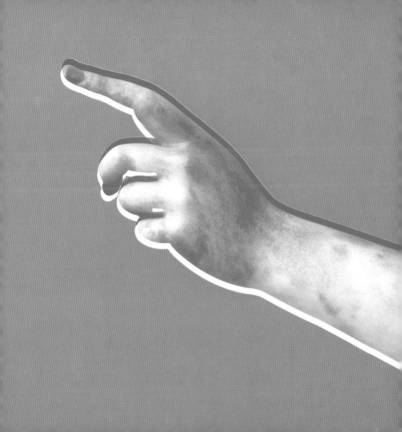

get out of here!

Because we are fearful and are unable to eradicate our fears, we get angry. Anger is a way of making us feel better and less afraid. That's why inadequate people become bullies. It's easy to be angry. It's easy to get addicted to the adrenalin and to need that rush to make you feel okay. It is hard to stop anger and, like all other emotions, if you try to suppress it, you'll only make it worse. The Buddhist way is not to attach to emotions. It is just anger, it is not your anger. You don't have to hang on to it. If you examine it calmly it will, like all the other thoughts that pass through your mind, disappear.

mistakes

Never be afraid to make mistakes.
If you never make a mistake it's
unlikely you'll make anything else.

233

passions

A man who has not passed
through the inferno of his passions
has never overcome them.

C.G. JUNG

234

the long journey

A journey of a thousand miles begins with a single step.

235

the absurdity of Zen

Some think Zen merely absurd. Yet this absurdity is far better than the ignorance of those who find it absurd.

236

mirror

Do not seek to impose yourself on the world. Be like a mirror: when red comes, you are red, when blue comes you are blue. What good would a mirror be otherwise?

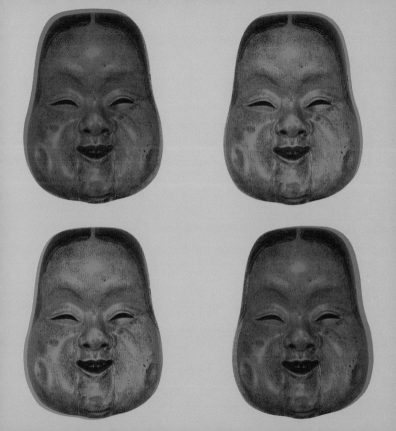

237

you're being followed!

If a man speaks or acts with an evil thought, pain follows him, as the wheel follows the foot of the ox that draws the cart; if a man speaks or acts with a pure thought, happiness follows him, as a shadow that never leaves him.

DHAMAPADA

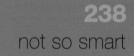

238

not so smart

Intelligence is merely
the shadow of truth.
How can the shadow
compete with the light?

239

dharma

Though I handed down mind's dharma, how can dharma be dharma? For neither mind nor dharma can really exist. Only thus can you understand the dharma that is passed with mind to mind.

DARUMA

240

throw it out!

As soon as you have accomplished something, throw it away! If you don't and let yourself become proud of your achievement, then you'll carry it around like a ball and chain. It is good to achieve but, once you've done it, pass on to the next thing.

241

using your light wisely

Meditation only helps if it is accompanied by right understanding. Meditation without understanding is like using a flashlight to search for something in the wrong room. If that was not so, then every frog would be a Buddha.

stop right now

Self-justification is worse
than the crime.

243

shhhh!

Don't talk unless you
can improve the silence.

ANONYMOUS

244

true worth

If a gem falls into the mud it is still valuable. But if dust should ascend to heaven it is still worthless.

SAADI OF SHIRAZ

245

the fire sermon

Buddha said: "Everything is on fire, the eye is on fire, forms are on fire, eye-consciousness is on fire, the impressions received by the eye are on fire. ...And with what are these things on fire? With the fires of lust, anger, and illusion."

no want of desire

Man never has what he wants, because what
he wants is everything.

C-F RAMUZ

247

jackdaw and jackass

How we laugh at the jackdaw that steals bright, shiny objects for which it has no use. And how we love to copy him.

248

the way

No one is ever lost on a straight path.

no exit

Is there no way out of the mind?

SYLVIA PLATH

250

a state of mind

Meditation is hard because you cannot achieve
it by effort alone. It is not like concentration, a
sort of mental muscle building. In meditation
you have to relax your mind in a special way.
Normally as soon as you start to feel sufficiently
relaxed, you go to sleep. In meditation this is a
no-no. But just look at a frog on his lily pad. He
can stay motionless all day, but he's not asleep,
as any passing fly will discover to its cost.

251

it's good to fall

I don't like people who haven't fallen or stumbled.
Their virtue is lifeless and isn't of much value. Life hasn't
revealed its beauty to them.

BORIS PASTERNAK

emotive thoughts

When anger finds you in one place—move!
Emotions may rise up anywhere but you don't
have to give in to them.

unforgiving

There is no forgiveness in Buddhism. It's not through lack of compassion; it's just that no one, not even Buddha, has the right to forgive. If you make a mistake, you'll bear the consequences now or later. Then pick yourself up, learn from your mistake, and carry on.

254

understanding

Understanding is better than money. You have to look after money, but understanding will look after you.

255

the benefits of age

The beautiful become vain and the strong
become violent. What use is it to speak of
the Way to such people? He who is not
yet turning gray will make mistakes if he
as much as speaks of the Way; how much
less can he put it into practice!

LIEH-TZU

256

clear thinking

Logic is great for certain processes, but quite useless for others. We need to use all our mental tools to build anything worthwhile. What would you think of a carpenter who only used a hammer?

257

deeds

Everyone knows it is much
harder to turn word into deed
than deed into word.

MAXIM GORKY

258
certain doubts

If a man will begin with certainties, he shall end
in doubts; but if he will be content to begin with
doubts, he shall end in certainties.

FRANCIS BACON

259

famous last words

Zen masters often composed a death poem.
What would you say?

260

aging

As you get older remember that it is your mind, not your waist, which should continue to broaden.

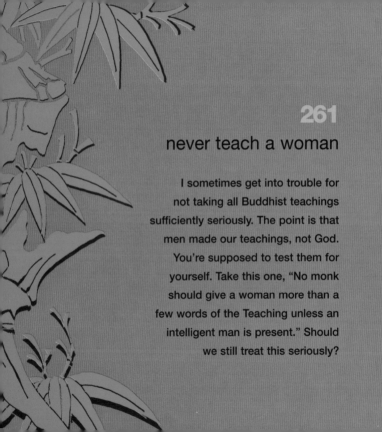

261

never teach a woman

I sometimes get into trouble for not taking all Buddhist teachings sufficiently seriously. The point is that men made our teachings, not God. You're supposed to test them for yourself. Take this one, "No monk should give a woman more than a few words of the Teaching unless an intelligent man is present." Should we still treat this seriously?

262
the demon drink

Contrary to what is sometimes written, Buddhists who indulge in alcohol do not become ravening beasts, they just become tipsy Buddhists.

swan song

An angler spotted a swan with its head underwater apparently dabbling for food. Some time later he saw the bird still in the same position and grew curious. When he went to investigate he found that a giant pike had seized the swan by the head and tried to drag it under. The swan had resisted and the pike had refused to let go. In the end they had both died.

too many people

The quality of moral behavior varies in inverse ratio to
the number of human beings involved.

ALDOUS HUXLEY

satori

Imperturbable and serene, the ideal man practices no
virtues. Self-possessed and dispassionate, he commits no
sin. Calm and silent, he gives up seeing and hearing. Even
and upright, his mind abides nowhere.

HUI-NENG

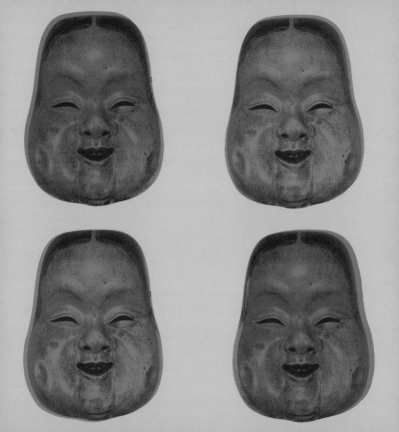

266

drifting clouds

All sorts of thoughts pass through your mind. When they are good thoughts people claim credit for them ("That was my bright idea!"), when they are bad thoughts people feel guilty about having them ("Why am I so jealous?"). Just sit and observe your thoughts. Don't try to own them but let them arise and disappear just like clouds in an otherwise blue sky. This is sometimes called "insight meditation" and it helps you to become familiar with the workings of the mind. Be a mind tourist.

offensive behavior

For some people the only purpose of having religious
convictions is the pleasure of being offended by those who
do not share them. You would hope that this did not apply
to Buddhists but, alas, you would hope in vain.

problems

Among all my patients in the second half of life—that is to
say over 35—there has not been one whose problem in the
last resort was not that of finding a religious outlook on life.

C.G. JUNG

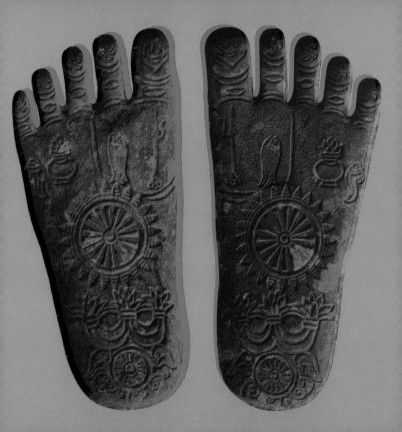

269

I hate you!

Buddhists believe in hell. Not the Christian hell, a place of eternal punishment, but in the many hells of the mind. If you hang on to "your" anger, if you start to own it, then it festers and turns into hate. Once you hate, you are in hell. The object of your hate will almost certainly reciprocate your hatred and, there you are, both of you stuck in a situation that is increasingly hard to break free from. The hells of the mind are far more fearful than any storybook nonsense dreamed up by our ancestors because you are not kept in these hells by demons but by your own worst enemy, yourself.

270
happiness

To give happiness is good; to exchange it is better.

271

dhana

Blessed are those who can
give without remembering and
take without forgetting.

272

insufficient merit

The Emperor told Daruma of all his great religious works. He has endowed temples, given money for the upkeep of monks and nuns, had sutras chanted and paid for huge temple bells. "How much merit have I accumulated?" he asked. "None at all," replied Daruma.

the nature of fear

The elephant that fears a
mouse may brave a tiger.

weeds

A weed is a plant whose virtues
have not been discovered.

eyes wide open

Some people choose to meditate with their eyes open. One reason is that what is going to happen will be right here and now. If you close your eyes you may enter various types of trance state and, though these can be very pleasant, they are not productive. Buddhism isn't about floating away on a pretty pink cloud. Nirvana isn't a place in the sky. It all happens right here, right now.

276

yak talk

As a yak-cow, when the hairs of her tail become entangled in anything, would rather suffer death than injury to her tail, even so should you keep to your duty—as the yak to her tail.

BUDDHA

277

greed

You would expect that students of Buddhism are not susceptible to greed for money or possessions. But there are other forms of greed. What about spiritual gain? It is possible to be so intent upon making progress that you become as greedy as any money-obsessed businessman. To be greedy in this way is no less damaging.

searching for the way

If you are lost and trying to get home and meet a man who says, "Follow me, I know the way!" you would do well to follow him. But if you are seeking enlightenment and someone says, "Follow me, I know the way," you can rely on it that he is also lost.

279

tell truth and shame the devil

Right Speech includes a duty not to tell lies.

perceptions

Bad people often seem interesting and good ones seem boring. This tells us something about the people involved and a lot about ourselves.

buddha nature

Buddhism has always had a great affinity with nature. This is not just about compassion (though Buddhist temples do have a great tendency to collect every stray animal for miles around). In Zen it is said that even the grass and stones will become enlightened. Even St. Francis, for all his preaching to the birds, did not go that far. Not only does everything have Buddha nature, but everything *is* Buddha nature—including nature.

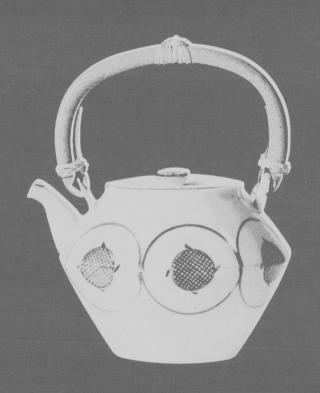

282
evil

What we call evil is simply
ignorance bumping its head in the dark.

HENRY FORD

283
changing

Anyone can change. Change is natural. Changing for the
better is another matter altogether.

mindfulness

Right Mindfulness is part of the Noble Eightfold Path that all Buddhists are supposed to follow. It is often misunderstood and confused with concentration. Mindfulness isn't an uptight I-want-to-shut-everything-out feeling. On the contrary, you can be mindful and still fully aware of everything that goes on around you. Being mindful is to fully engage with your activity so that it becomes an expression of your true self. That is one reason why, for example, the tea ceremony has close links to Zen.

285

concentration

Right Concentration is another strand
of the Noble Eightfold Path. Try this:
take a favorite Buddha image and
look at it carefully for a minute or so.
Now close your eyes and try to retain
the picture of the Buddha in your mind.
If you haven't done this before it won't stay
long. Try again, and again. If you practice
regularly you'll find that your
concentration improves enormously.

it's mad to be different

Zen, in particular, is regularly accused of being a form of madness. If you believe that people who think differently are mad, then it is true that Zen Buddhists are all total nutcases. However, all Buddhists are peaceful folk who want nothing but good for their fellow humans. The way they express their beliefs may seem odd but, in a world that countenances slaughter, famine, poverty, and disease, you would be justified in wondering who are the mad ones. Zen seeks to liberate us from the shackles of thought that enslave us. To do that it uses some highly original and unconventional means. But our usual way of thinking is a deeply ingrained habit and it takes some serious shock tactics to help us break free.

is this a poem?

Colorless green ideas sleep furiously. Noam Chomsky invented this sentence to demonstrate the gap between grammatical structure and meaning. It has rather a haiku quality to it. Chomsky would be furious.

stupid answer

A student had been working on the koan, "What is the sound of one hand clapping?" One day another student was being interviewed by the master on his progress with the same koan. Normally such interviews are confidential but, in this case they were overheard. "What is your answer?" asked the master. The student struck the floor hard with his palm. The master smiled, "I see you have penetrated the koan," he said. The eavesdropper waited and, when it was his turn to visit the master, he also hit the floor with his palm. "You fool!" shouted the master, "you understand nothing at all!"

289
one god

One of the things I like about the Far East is the lack of
religious monopolies. In the United States or Europe you
are born into or join one religion and that's it, probably for
life. A Japanese may be a Buddhist but will also have
deep respect for Confucius and Shinto. A Chinese
person will be able to accommodate Confucianism and
Taoism alongside Buddhism. In Thailand no one would
think it odd for a devout Buddhist to make offerings at
the shrine for spirits that protect the household. This
easygoing attitude has not only made for greater religious
harmony but has allowed one set of beliefs to enrich
others and, in turn, to be enriched by them.

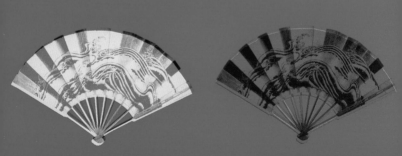

dog

A Zen master was traveling with his pupil
when a fierce dog began to bark at him.
"How dare you assault my master!" cried
the pupil.
"The dog is more consistent than you are,"
observed the master. "He barks at everyone
alike because it is in his nature. You think of
me as your master and yet remain quite
oblivious to the qualities of others."

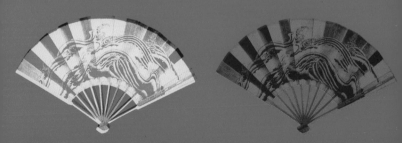

291
traveling happily

Happiness is not a destination, it's a manner
of traveling.

292

the mind

The true nature of the mind is empty, clear, and radiant.

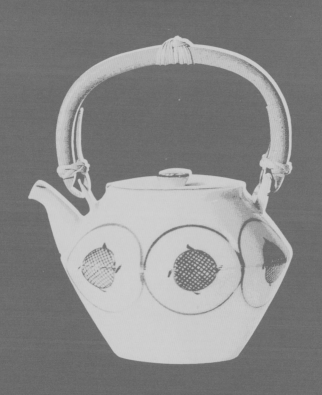

293
fighting dirty

Miyamoto Musashi was the most famous and feared swordsman in Japanese history. He spent the first fifty years of his life studying the Way of the Sword and was successful in many hundreds of fights. Yet so concerned was he about the sudden attack of an enemy that he never dared take a bath in case he was caught unawares.

chatter

Words are men's daughters, but God's sons are things.

SAMNUEL MADDEN

don't wait for tomorrow

It's no good waiting for retirement to "make
the most of life." Start today!

pleasure versus pain

Pleasures shallow, sorrows deep.

CHINESE SAYING

297

benefits of philosophy

A philosopher is a man who knows exactly what to do until it happens to him.

298

the working of the way

Turning back is how the Way moves and weakness is the method it employs.

LAO-TZU

299
love and hate

Thinking, "I like this, I hate that," is a great hindrance. To take everything as it comes without discrimination is the trick.

300

heaven on earth

Earth is a paradise, the only one we will ever know. We will realize it the moment we open our eyes. We don't have to make it a paradise—it is one. We only have to make ourselves fit to inhabit it.

HENRY MILLER

301

the eight nos

No production or destruction; no annihilation
nor persistence; no unity nor plurality; no coming
in nor going out.

MADHYAMIKA SASTRA

302

no secrets

See with your eyes and hear with
your ears. Nothing in the world is hidden.
What would you have me say?

TENKEI

303

late starter

It is never too late to start on the Buddhist path. The Zen master Joshu did not start to study until he was sixty. He became enlightened at eighty, and went on to become one of the greatest of all Zen teachers.

304

beauty isn't everything

The horse is praised for its speed and beauty, though it
tires quickly. The camel is derided for its ungainly
appearance but it works tirelessly.

305

farm sense

Even the best soil, if not skillfully farmed,
will bring forth nothing but weeds.

306
mountaineers

When climbing Everest it's best not to
be in a hurry.

307
building

With people it's always better to build bridges than fences.

riding the carousel

Would you like another chance at life? Be honest. The aim of Buddhism is to escape the wheel of life and end the pain of existence. How many of us are really ready to leave life behind? How many lives are so painful you wouldn't want another one? I've never seen any convincing evidence that rebirth happens, though it fits very conveniently with the law of karma. But just because something makes a good theory doesn't make it true. Let's assume that it really happens. I can just imagine losing one body and being only too keen to find another. For many people I imagine that the wheel of life is really a carousel, they can't wait for another turn. That is probably a good reason why the road to enlightenment is such a long one.

warming to the work

Chopping your own wood warms you twice.

310
real hunger

A painting of a rice cake will not
satisfy hunger.

CHINESE SAYING

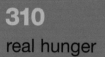

danse macabre

In our society death is the ultimate taboo. People are talking quite seriously of scientific advances that will allow us to live, if not forever, then at least for much, much longer than ever before. What sort of society would this be? One that is stagnant, one in which no growth is possible. For growth only comes from death. Life and death are not two things, they are one. That is why the Hindus saw Shiva as both the Creator and Destroyer. We recoil from death but we are foolish to do so. When the time is right, we should embrace it as a true friend.

god and me

My "Me" is God, nor do I recognize any other Me
except my God Himself.

ST. CATHERINE OF GENOA

the helpful dead

The dead don't die. They look on and help.

D.H. LAWRENCE

314

time to die

A son must go where his parents tell him. Nature is no other than my parents. If nature bids me die quickly and I object, what sort of son am I?

CHUANG-TZU

history is bunk

The past and future do not exist. There is
only now and that is what there always has
been and always will be.

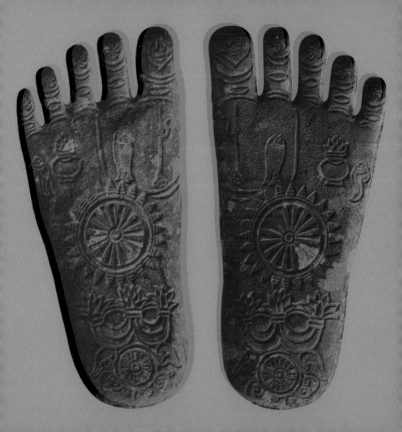

316
cold comfort

Religion is the frozen thought of
men out of which they build temples.

KRISHNAMURTI

317

no religion

Everyone in the ordinary world is
asleep. The religion of the familiar world is
mere emptiness; it's not religion at all.

SUFI SAYING

318

the answer

What is the secret? Vast emptiness
and nothing holy anywhere.

it's not a prize

Many religions believe that good behavior earns some sort of reward, either in this life or the next. This is wrong understanding. Moral behavior is a by-product of your understanding. As your meditation progresses your understanding deepens. Moral behavior is like the spots of measles, merely a symptom, not the cause.

320

breathing

People often find it hard to understand why watching your breath while meditating has any value or significance. Certainly it has no resemblance to Western ideas of religion but is widely practiced throughout the East. Some assume that it's just an exercise, or maybe something to do with yoga. It takes time to understand that breath is much more than just filling your lungs with oxygen. In fact breathing is quite literally at the heart of Buddhism. But to understand why, you must practice hard and long.

teachers

Even the best teachers can
only point the way. They cannot
make the journey for you

self-defeating

It is hard to bring down an adversary without
rolling in the muck yourself.

323

free man

I will not serve God like a laborer expecting payment.

RABIA EL-ADAWIA

324

buddha's advice to his son

"Whatever the form, Rahula, be it past, present or future, inward or outward, gross or subtle, high or low, near or far, every form must be regarded as it really is: 'This is not mine, not this am I, this is not the Self of me.'"

325

the middle way

Even moderation ought not to be practiced to excess.

going to the devil bit by bit

Wrongdoing is insidious and incremental. It is easy to think, "It's only a little thing, it won't matter," but it all mounts up. Eventually people who make a habit of wrongdoing find themselves trapped by it and unable to break out.

327

wisdom

Education may be forgotten but wisdom
remains to be found.

the advantages of celibacy

Why are holy men so often celibate? How many men are considered wise by their wife?

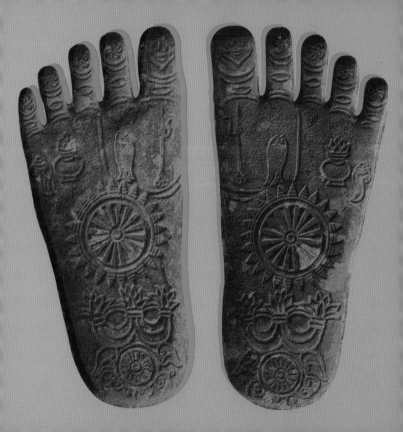

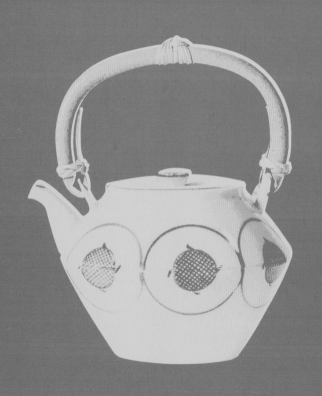

music from adversity

A kettle only starts to sing when it's up to its neck in hot water.

why are we here?

As far as we can discern, the sole purpose of human existence is to kindle a light in the darkness of mere being.

C.G. JUNG

sloth and torpor

A Buddhist abbot once gave me a pamphlet on basic teachings. One of the things it warned against was Sloth and Torpor, which sounded like a couple of giant slobs vegetating out in front of the TV with a six-pack. Even so, the pamphlet had a point. Buddhism isn't just a part-time activity. Understanding comes in its own sweet time, but for it to come at all takes real effort on your part.

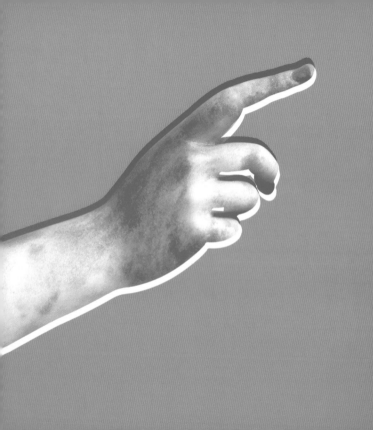

the child is father to the man

Many Buddhists not only believe in rebirth but also think
it happens so quickly that people who are children now
may be your parents next time around. Doesn't that
make you look at kids in a whole new way?

the natural course

We cannot hold back the blooming
of the flowers or the flow of the stream.
Eventually, all things reach fruition.

LOY CHING-YUEN

334
death

There are no dead.

MAURICE MAETERLINK

335
mindfulness

Ask yourself without ceasing, "What is the essence of this mind?"

on being important

In Japan the emperors were supplanted by military dictators called shoguns. The emperor was persuaded that he was too important for mundane affairs. In fact he was so important that he was actually holy and, therefore able to do nothing mundane. Other people did the "menial" tasks (like ruling the entire country), while the emperor played. It's easy to become just too important.

337

seeing karma

As your meditation makes progress you find it easier and easier to see other people's karma (seeing your own is much harder). As a compassionate person you would like to intercede to prevent disaster. Be aware that it is never easy to do so and you might just make things worse. Telling someone ugly facts they are not ready to understand is a road to disaster.

338

virtue and vice

Search others for
virtues. Search yourself
for vices.

339

getting in the swim

All religions can cite examples of believers who showed great courage, both moral and physical, but Buddhism requires a special sort of courage. Letting go and floating freely on the stream of life is the hardest thing to do. It's a bit like learning to swim, you need confidence that something as wet and weak as water will actually hold you up and not let you drown. Much of modern civilization is devoted to the proposition that life is dangerous and can only be handled by keeping it at bay behind protective barriers. Can you really step out from behind them and trust yourself to float on the stream?

conceptual thinking

As apes spend their time throwing things away and picking them up again, so it is with learning. Just give up all this learning. Forget about words such as "ignorant," "enlightened," "pure," "impure," "great," "little," and "attachment." These are merely concepts. Give them up!

HUANG PO

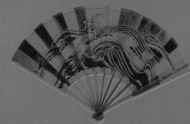

341
flowers

When you look at a flower, at a color, without naming it, without like or dislike, without any screen between you and the thing you see as a flower, without the word, without thought, then the flower has an extraordinary color and beauty. But when you...say: "This is a rose," you have already conditioned your response.

J. KRISHNAMURTI

342

a sense of loss

How do I know that love of life is not merely a delusion? Maybe one who dreads to die is just like a little child who has lost his way and can't find his home.

CHUANG-TZU

cynics

Beware attempts by others to blow you off course. People who know no better see Buddhism as irrational and full of "mysticism" (a term they misunderstand). They'll appeal to you to be "sensible" and "normal." But it is they, not you, who have the problem. Buddhism offers no harm to anyone. Those who would try to persuade you to give it up do not have your best interests at heart.

fragile body, firm mind

Man, whose body is as fragile as a jar, should make his thoughts firm as a fortress.

DHAMAPADA

respect

Over the centuries respect for Buddha has led to some very silly developments that obscure the real nature of Buddhism. Images are treated with huge reverence, stored in a high place, and only touched with the greatest care. Some of them are even said to have miraculous properties. Why? These images are just painted wood, metal, and stone. They have nothing to do with Buddhism. If Buddha were around to see all this nonsense he'd have a fit. When the Taliban blew up a couple of Buddha images there was great outrage. Well, maybe as historical artifacts they were of value, but as religious symbols they were just heaps of stone. Pretty temples and ornate images are all very well, but they're not Buddhism.

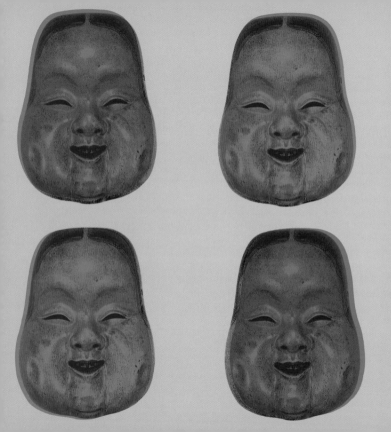

everyday

Your everyday mind is Zen.

CHAO-CHOU

god

All is God, and there is no God.

ZEN SAYING

mind matters

Gudo was Zen teacher to the emperor.
One day the emperor asked him whether
his everyday mind was really Buddha.
"If I say yes," replied Gudo, "you'll think
you understand something you do not. But
if I were to say no, I'd be contradicting a
fact known to many."

349

hard to grasp

If you long to be enlightened, you do not know what you long for. Look for the enlightenment you have already.

no going back

Once you take up Buddhism, and especially if you start to meditate, you will find that you have begun a path on which there is no going back. You may give up on Buddhism, but it will never give up on you. When you are in need, you will find that everything is still there waiting for you and, wonder of wonders, your understanding has deepened while you were away.

fundamental buddhist beliefs

In 1891 Colonel H.S. Olcott identified fourteen fundamental Buddhist beliefs, which remain a useful reference for anyone wanting to know what Buddhism is all about.

1. show tolerance

Buddhists should show the same tolerance, forbearance, and brotherly love to all men, without distinction, and an unswerving kindness toward members of the animal kingdom.

2. believe in evolution

Buddhists believe that the universe was evolved, not created, and it functions according to law, not according to the caprice of any god.

3. follow the teachings of the buddhas

The truths upon which Buddhism is founded are natural and have, Buddhists believe, been taught in successive kalpas (world periods) by illuminated beings called Buddhas. The name Buddha means "enlightened."

4. honour the wisdom of buddha

The fourth Teacher in the present kalpa was Sakya Muni, or Gautama Buddha, who was born in a royal family in India about 2,500 years ago. His name was Siddartha Gautama (and he was the founder of Buddhism).

5. escape rebirth by destroying ignorance

Sakya Muni taught that ignorance produces desire. Unsatisfied desire is the cause of rebirth, and rebirth the cause of sorrow. To get rid of sorrow it is necessary to escape rebirth; to escape rebirth it is necessary to extinguish desire, and to extinguish desire it is necessary to destroy ignorance.

6. banish the illusions of ignorance

Ignorance fosters the belief that rebirth is a necessary thing. When ignorance is destroyed the worthlessness of every such rebirth, considered as an end in itself, is perceived, as well as the paramount need for adopting a course of life by which the necessity of such repeated births can be abolished. Ignorance also produces the illusive and illogical idea that there is only one existence for man, and that this one life is followed by states of unchangeable pleasure or torment.

358

7. here's how

To dispel ignorance practice an all-embracing altruism in conduct, develop your intelligence and wisdom in thought, and rid yourself of desire.

8. receive life through death

Rid yourself of the desire to live, which is the cause of rebirth, to achieve Nirvana (the highest state of peace) through meditation.

9. meditate

To achieve spiritual enlightenment, or the development of that Buddha-like faculty which is latent in every human, you need to practice Right Meditation.

10. understand the four noble truths

Sakya Muni taught that ignorance can be dispelled and sorrow removed by knowledge of the Four Noble Truths, viz:

1. The miseries of existence.
2. The cause productive of misery, which is the desire ever renewed of satisfying oneself without ever being able to secure that end.
3. The destruction of that desire, or the estranging of oneself from it.
4. The means of obtaining this destruction of desire... (the Noble Eightfold Path) Right Belief, Right Thought, Right Speech, Right Action, Right Livelihood, Right Exertion, Right Remembrance, Right Meditation.

362

11. aim high

The essence of Buddhism as
summed up by the Tathagata
(Buddha) himself is:
To cease from all sin,
To get virtue,
To purify the heart.

12. believe in karma

The universe is subject to natural causation called "karma." The merits and demerits of a being in past existences determine one's condition in the present one. Each human being, therefore, has prepared the causes of effects that they now experience.

13. follow the laws

The obstacles to attainment of good karma may
be removed using the following Precepts:
1. Kill not;
2. Steal not;
3. Indulge in no forbidden sexual pleasures;
4. Lie not;
5. Take no intoxicating or stupefying drug or liquor.

14. believe only what you know

Buddhism discourages
superstitious credulity.
Gautama Buddha taught it to be
the duty of a parent to educate their
child in science and
literature. He also
taught that no one should
believe what is spoken by any sage,
written in any book, or affirmed by
tradition, unless it accord with reason.

Copyright © MQ Publications Ltd 2003

TEXT © Robert Allen 2003
ILLUSTRATIONS danny@dogtag.uk.com
DESIGN balley design associates

6th Avenue Books™ are published by
Time Warner Trade Publishing
1271 Ave. of the Americas
New York, NY 10020

Visit our Web site at www.twbookmark.com

An AOL Time Warner Company

Printed in China
First printing: 10 9 8 7 6 5 4 3 2 1

ISBN: 1-931722-23-4